HOW BIG
WAS A
DINOSAUR?

Additional design by Nicola Butler
With thanks to Darren Naish for information about dinosaurs

First published in 2011 by Usborne Publishing Ltd, 83-85 Saffron Hill, London ECIN 8RT, England.
www.usborne.com Copyright © 2011 Usborne Publishing Ltd.

HOW BIG
WAS A
DINOSAUR?

Anna Milbourne

Illustrated by Serena Riglietti

Designed by Laura Wood

Pipkin was a very small penguin
who was always asking
very big questions.

"Where do flowers come from?"

"How do birds fly?"

"What's inside
our world?"

But the thing he wanted to know MOST of all was:
"How **big** was a dinosaur?"

Pipkin's Mama said, "To answer that you'd have to go back to a time before penguins or people, or cities or snow..."

"...when the world was all
warm and covered in forests."

"Alright," said Pipkin,
and he did just that...

A group of little creatures
scuttled through the trees.

"Excuse me," said Pipkin.
"How big is a dinosaur?"

"I'm a dinosaur," said one of the creatures,
"and I'm THIS big."

"Are you the biggest one?"
asked Pipkin.

"No," said the dinosaur.
"I'm not as big as HIM..."

A fast, snappy creature
dashed through the trees.

"Excuse me," said Pipkin.
"How big is a dinosaur?"

"I'm a dinosaur,"
the creature snapped,
"and I'm THIS big."

"Are you the biggest one?" asked Pipkin.

"No," said the dinosaur.
"I'm not as big as HER..."

A gnashing, slashing
creature crashed
through the trees.

"E-e-excuse me," said Pipkin.
"How big is a dinosaur?"

"I'm a dinosaur,"
the creature roared,
"and I'm THIS big."

"You are rather big," said Pipkin.
"And you have very big teeth..."

"...but you're not
as big as HIM."

A stomping, clomping creature
marched across the plains.

"Excuse me," said Pipkin.
"How big is a dinosaur?"

"I'm a dinosaur," the creature boomed, "and I'm THIS BIG."

"Are you the biggest one?"
asked Pipkin.

"Yes," said the dinosaur. "I'm...
AS BIG AS BIG
CAN BE!"

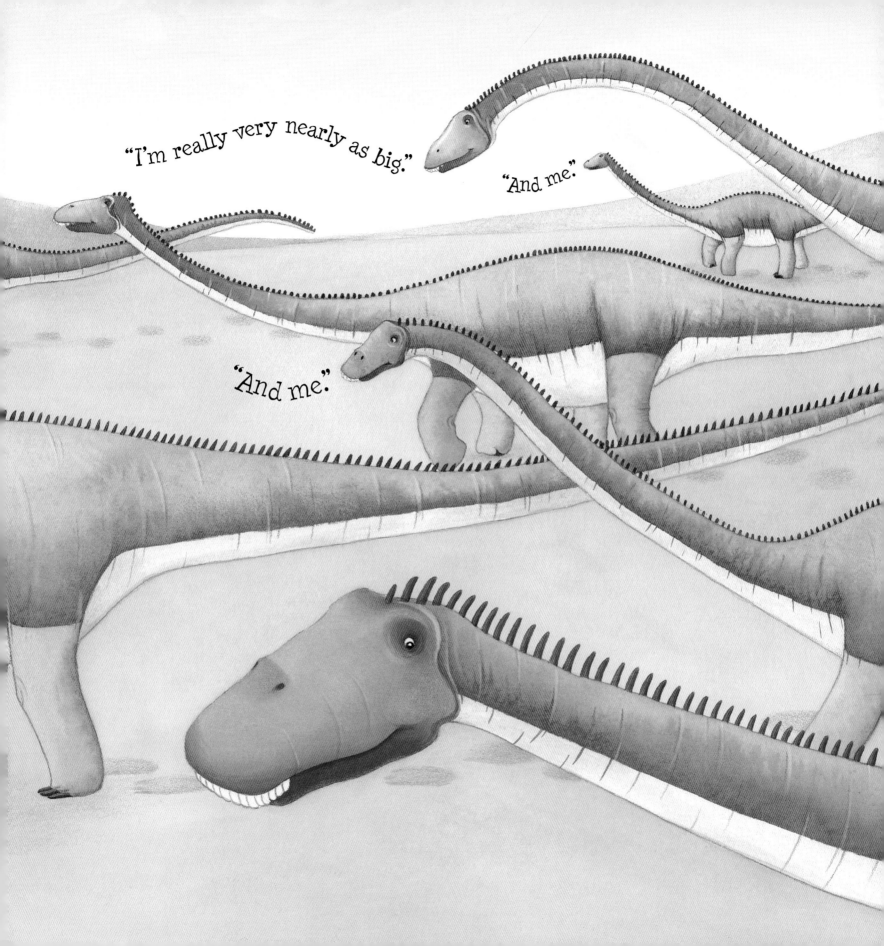

When Pipkin came home, he said to his Mama:
"There were all KINDS of different dinosaurs:
groups of little scuttling ones,
and bigger rushing, snapping ones,
and even bigger roary ones with very big teeth.

But the biggest dinosaur of them all
was longer than long and taller than tall...
AS BIG AS BIG
CAN BE.

"Mama, do you think I'll ever grow as big as a dinosaur?" Pipkin asked.

"Eat up your dinner, my little Pip," Mama said, "and we shall see."

Come this way to see some really **big** dinosaurs.